A PILL TO BEAUTIFUL LIFE

Gosa Tharani

Presentation by *BookLeaf Publishing*

Web: www.bookleafpub.com

E-mail: info@bookleafpub.com

ISBN: 978-93-95223-64-5

First edition 2022

DEDICATION

This is the first book as an author that I dedicate to my family, friends, my brother, and sisters. And everyone I met who gave this experience to have a thought.

ACKNOWLEDGEMENT

Success is defined by your own thoughts...
Beauty exists in your thoughts...
Beauty exists in your words...
Beauty exists in you make people feel...
Beauty exists in loving, beauty exists in responsibility, beauty exists in happy hustling…

Special thanks and love to my mom.

PREFACE

Gmail: acos.stories@gmail.com
Insta: acos teller
Youtube: acos teller

Contents

1. Don't miss out

Don't miss out...
What can you do today?

Don't miss out...
Moments ..by overthinking.

Don't miss out...
Focus ..by distracting.

Don't miss out...
Life by trying to understand it.

Don't miss out...
The joy of living blissfully.

Don't miss out...
The life you can live.

Don't miss out...
The small things that make you happy.

Don't miss out...
The child in you.

Don't miss out...
The responsibility to love and take care.

Don't miss out...
Today by thinking about tomorrow.

Don't miss out ...
This day to work, to find out a way, to get up
and to run.

2. Learn it now

"Learn to know your thoughts and your
emotions ".

Learn it now...
To control your thoughts.

Learn it now...
To know your emotions.

Learn it now...
To mind your thoughts.

Learn it now...
To face your emotions.

Learn it now...
To see what's happening around and within.

Learn it now...
To react or to respond.

Learn it now...
 Be patient.

Learn it now...
To focus.

Learn it now...
To know your potential and try your best.

Learn it now...
To be grateful.

3. Never give up

Never give up on a relationship you believe in
…You may end up with surprises.

Never give up on your dreams...
Because they make your life meaningful.

Never give up on the problems…
Find out the solutions.

Never give up on the people and come to the
conclusions...
Have a conversation.

Never give up because somebody has an opinion
on you...
You know yourself better than anybody else.

So live your life.

4. Let them be jealous

If it is living your dream…
Then let them be jealous.

If it is a matter of your happiness…
Then let them be jealous.

If it is a question of your strength and
resilience…
Then let them be jealous.

If it is a matter of your honor…
Then let them be jealous.

If it is a choice of people you want in your life...
Then let them be jealous.

5. Walk away

Walk away if you feel avoided.
Walk away if you become unbearable.
Walk away to accept the truth.
Walk away to accept the mistakes.
Walk away to understand what's happening
within.
Walk away to come back with a solution.
Walk away to love more without judging.
Walk away to look at the world differently.
Walk away to change...

6. Leave

8

Leave it free
Let it go…
Leave legacy
Let it follow…
Leave knowledge
Let it spread.
Leave beauty
Let it glow.
Leave love
Let it spread…
Leave your smile
Let it give you happiness.
Leave your thoughts
Let it give you freedom…

. 7. How long can I sustain it??

If there is always confusion about how long can
I sustain in one such job??
When there is a question of how long?
Then remember nobody's life is a guarantee.
Find out a plan, find out a way.
It always comes with the question of how do you
want to see yourself in your life.
If you are not understanding the future then take
that one step forward one at a time with
whatever you are having.
But take that one step.
You are not the job, do you?
Your job is just a part of you!!! A life that gives
you the experience of learning, earning, saving,
trying, and negotiating with the things, money,
and people in this world.
You and I are having different jobs but always
remember we are one with different stories. So
make sure you own your story.
Your job needs your time.

8. Don't let worry take away your today

No guilt.
No regret.
No worry.
No stress.
The story was not the same and will not be the same.
A promise of hope.
A promise of trust.
A promise of cherishing good memories.
A promise of love.
A promise of forgiveness.
A promise of being at peace.
A promise of work.
A promise of fully living your today.
Live, love and laugh.

9. What happens??

What happens if it is messy..
What happens if you did a mistake.
What happens if there are judgments..
What happens if there is change…
Let it be, let it go, let it come..

10. Yes you matter

Did you matter?
Yes, you matter...
Yes, your dreams matter...
Yes, your pain matters...
Yes, your goals matter...
Yes, your failures matter...
Yes, your questions matter...
Yes, your answers matter...
Yes, your fight matters...
Yes, your decision matter...
Yes, accepting mistakes of yours matters...
Yes, you matter.

11. Be brave to accept whatever you are feeling..

Life is simple..don't make it a mess...

Go focus, earn, work hard, love, learn, accept and run.
Believe that you will be amazing..which attracts you towards the eternity of being happy and strong.
so be brave to accept whatever and however, you are, and don't be scared of the change you wanted in your life.

12. Miss them

It is as important as to miss them as you love
them.
Because we often forget the boundaries, become
possessive and become abundant in their lives
which starts taking away their freedom …
Miss them for a while,
Miss them to know that you love them the most.
Miss them to tell that …do whatever makes you
happy, you still love and care for them.
Miss it for a while…see what will you get
back…

13. Don't expect the life you want…

Because your life will be a whole lot of surprises
and unplanned situations no matter how hard
you try.

You may be very successful in your
career...maybe you planned this.
But if you are so serious about everything
happening around you ,then you come up with a
roller coaster of emotions that doesn't let you
think how far you have come.

It starts breaking down your self-confidence and
you won't care to think of yourself and all the
milestones you have reached till now….
Because when any of these plans are not
happening your way…you get disappointed and
that disappointment leads to disaster…

Learn to be adaptable.

When it's time to face such situations then
don't forget to remember where did you start
from.. how hard you have worked and the
obstacles you have crossed to reach here.

Don't be so   serious about life , the experiences
and the situations happening..
Try to look at the world as it is.

All you have in your hands is to find out the
solutions and keep working..

Let the results speak..

It's you who can motivate yourself to do it…not
by giving upon your physical and mental health
but by mindfully taking care of it as your
responsibility ,no matter what may be the
results…

Because only a happy mind and happy heart
will make you think   and make you successful..

Don't let anything hurt you so much...

Because everything is temporary and this too
shall pass…

Pray for the strength and where there is the
belief there is a way…

If this plan is not working…then there may be
something big waiting for you…

Look at life as it is…only thing you can do is to do your work and wait. Take responsibility for your health, your thoughts, and your environment. Hold back to those who love you…
Everything is temporary and this too shall pass…

14. A prayer

"Prayer without a deed is expecting a tree
without planting a seed".

Pray for the courage.
Pray for the power to work.
Pray for the good.
Pray that you are grateful for giving this life and
today.

"Pray for the strength and worship your deeds".

15. Make it happen!!

There is always another day...
But what if you miss this today by thinking, by
doing nothing, and lost in your thoughts...
Life just doesn't happen…make it happen.

16. #Live it

This moment passes.
This day passes..

People leave..
Dreams shatter..
And this becomes a story..

Before this moment passes…live it.
Before this day passes…live it.
Before the people leave…love them to the
fullest and live with them.
Before the dream shatters...find out a plan and
live your dream.
Live it by spending time with your loved ones
and by taking care of them.
Live it by enjoying your journey towards
achieving your dream.
Live it by dancing, singing, and playing until
your heart feels happy.
Live it by relishing the amazing food...
Live your life the way you want before you
leave this world.

17. This mind

This mind always tries to take control of you:
Don't let it take you.
This mind often tells you to give up: Don't give
up
This mind often tells you to be depressed: Don't
do it
This mind often tells you to be lazy: Get up and
move
This mind often tells you to deviate from the
people who cared about you because you are
busy: Tell them that you always have time for
that and you will give it to them and laugh out
loud with them.
This mind often tells you to be comfortable: If
that is not your vision then run.
This mind often tells you to hate: If you cannot
love then don't hate because it is taking away
the space.
This mind often tells you to forget: But
remember. Remember what made you and who
made you feel good and happy.

18. Freeze it, please!!

Can I freeze this moment?
Can I freeze these laughs??
Can I freeze this smile???
Can I freeze this love????
Can   I freeze this time?????
If I cannot!! Then please let me take a picture to
live with it and freeze it in my memories.

19. You won't cry again

For if you loved.
You won't cry again..

For if you are alone.
You won't cry again..

Don't let them see.

You won't cry again …
If you are not prepared for this goodbye.

You won't cry again...
For putting someone else before yourself.

Because you loved truly…
And not everyone can do this...
So you !! won't cry again…

20. Everybody told

My mom told: To fight.
My grandpa told: To pray.
My grandma told: To love.
My dad told: To worth your time.
My siblings told: To smile and dance my heart
out.

My friends told me: To live with memories.
My brother told: To treasure it because nobody
spoon feeds your life.
And I told: Thank you and I love you.

21. Have faith

The power of faith in the god
Gives you the energy to work harder.
The power to faith in the love
Gives you the shoulder to rely on any situations
you face.
The power of faith in the spirit
Doesn't make you alone in this world.
The power of faith in the work you do
Gets you there where you want to.

YOU ARE THE ONLY ONE WHO CAN
MAKE YOUR STORY. SOME CHAPTERS
MAY BE BORING AND DIFFICULT BUT
BELIEVE THERE IS ANOTHER CHAPTER
IN YOUR LIFE. MAKE AN EFFORT TO
TURN THAT PAGE. MAKE SURE YOU ARE
PROUD OF YOURSELF BEFORE YOU
LEAVE. GIVE SOME LOVE, HELP
SOMEONE, BE KIND AND FORGIVE.